IT'S THAT TIME OF YEAR! Holi IS HERE!

BY VANESSA KAPADIA

It's That Time of Year! Holi is Here!

Book 3 of the It's That Time of Year Series.

Copyright © 2023 by Vanessa Kapadia

All rights reserved. No part of this book may be reproduced, distributed, or transmitted in any form or by any means, including photocopying, recording, or other electronic or mechanical methods, without prior written permission of the author, except in the case of brief quotations embodied in critical articles and reviews and certain other non-commercial uses permitted by copyright law.

ISBN

978-0-6454876-6-4 (Paperback)

978-0-6454876-7-1 (Hardcover)

978-0-6454876-2-6 (Ebook)

Dedication

For my adorable nephew, Hayden. May you continue to spread joy with all the vibrancy of the colours of Holi.

Once a year there is a night and day,

when we get coloured powders to play.

To mark the end of the Indian winter and start of spring.

To spread the love and happiness the season brings.

It's That Time of Year!

Holi is Here!

During Holi we put our differences aside,
so that peace in our hearts can reside.
No matter who you are or where you come from,
everyone comes together, everyone does belong.

Holi starts on Purnima, when the moon is full,
hearts aglow, we perform the Holika Dahan ritual.
It's where the adults create Holika, a special fire,
the children stand a safe distance away and admire.
It symbolises evil being destroyed,
and good being saved, leaving everyone overjoyed.

Holika Dahan

How many items can you spot that are blue?

The next step is the Parikrama, performed under the moon's rays.

Walking in circles around the fire; a safe distance away.

Remembering to hold an adult's hand and walking carefully,

whilst the Holika creates a feeling of harmony.

It keeps us healthy by cleansing the air around,

to keep everyone safe and sound.

It's symbolic of leaving behind our negative thoughts and feelings,

so we can begin the new season with healing.

Parikrama

How many items can you spot that are pink?

The next day is when the fun starts,
bringing joy and happiness to our hearts.
We begin by wearing clothes of white,
or another colour which is light.

Kapada Paherva

How many items can you spot that are orange?

We hurry outside to play,
with different colours for the day.
We start the rainbow fun,
by repeating two words that are sung.

"Holi Hai!"
"Holi Hai!"

We chant before we begin,
followed by music so we can dance and spin.

Dhuleti

How many items can you spot that are red?

HOLI HAI!
HOLI HAI!

We then bring out special coloured powder called 'Gulal',

rubbed with care on your cheeks – or 'gaal',

So many colours and shades to be seen,

everything from red, yellow, blue to green.

Rang Lagavo

How many items can you spot that are yellow?

Just when we think we are done,

it's time for a new kind of fun.

Water and colour are infused,

placed in pichkaris to be used.

Once the festivities come to an end,

we clean up to rejoice with family and friends.

Holi Ramo

How many items can you spot that are purple?

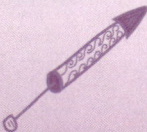

Want to learn more about other Hindu Festivals? Then check out other titles in the series:

'It's That Time of Year! Diwali is Here!' (Winner of the NYC Big Book Award 2022 - Children's Religion) for a fun and simple introduction to Diwali, the 'Festival of Lights.'

Learn about the festival and the rituals of the five days of Diwali. Don't forget to find all the hidden diyas along the way.

'It's That Time of Year! Raksha Bandhan is Here!' for a simple explanation of the rituals performed to celebrate the special bond between siblings.

Don't forget to find all the hidden Rakhris along the way.

For more details on the book series and upcoming releases be sure to checkout the series website:

www.itsthattimeofyearseries.com

www.ingramcontent.com/pod-product-compliance
Lightning Source LLC
Chambersburg PA
CBRC090836010526
44107CB00051B/1638